Tiny House

The Definitive Manual To Tiny Houses: Home Construction, Interior Design, Tiny House Living

Mason Algarotti

Introduction

I want to thank you and congratulate you for grabbing this book, *"Tiny House: The Definitive Manual To Tiny Houses: Home Construction, Interior Design, Tiny House Living"*.

This book is the ultimate definitive manual to tiny houses.

I personally believe that the tiny house movement is one of the best things to have happened to the average American's financial and economic potentials and why do I say so?

Take a look at these statistics:

- Most Americans spend 50-75% of the income that they earn throughout their lifetime, on putting a roof over their heads. This basically means that an average American spends at least 15 years worth of his income on building or renting a home that he can live on. If you doubt this statistic, read this article on CBS news for more information on this.

Now you would agree with me that most people's idea of a dream home is something really big with dozens of rooms and spaces that they would hardly even use. So why sacrifice so much, spend so much and hurt yourself financially for something you do not need.

Let us look at the statistics based on surveys carried out on people who have joined the tiny house movement:

- Up to 68% of tiny house owners don't have mortgage.

- Up to 55% of all tiny home owners in the country have more savings in the bank than the average American.

- 78% of tiny house owners fully own their houses.

- The average cost of building a tiny house is about $23,000 while the average American home would cost an average of $272,000.

All of these statistics lend credence to the fact that tiny houses can help to solve a lot of financial challenges that majority of Americans are facing these days.

This book is a thorough guide that contains step by step tips on how to join the tiny house movement. It will teach how to prepare for your tiny home, how to build, design and decorate your tiny home as well as how to make your living comfortable and enjoyable.

Thanks again for reading this book, I hope you enjoy it!

Table of Contents

Chapter 1: History of Tiny House Movements

The sizes of homes in America have grown exponentially over the last fifty years. In the 1800's and the early 1900's, the sizes of homes were about 800- 1,000 square feet as houses were designed for usability and would usually be big enough to house a family with few kids. Nowadays however, an average American is about 2,600 square feet in size. This growth in size was traced to an increase in material wealth and a need to show off wealth and prestige. As people grew richer, they felt the need to show off their increasing financial status by building houses that were larger than everyone else's. So houses grew from an average of 1,000 square feet in the early 1900's to an average of 1,780 square feet in 1978, 2,479 in 2007 and 2,662 in 2013.

The most interesting thing about this growth in home sizes is that as the homes grew larger, the sizes of families grew smaller. People were no longer birthing 6, 7 kids; an average of four kids was the trend. So I'm tempted to ask? What were the larger spaces for?

There have been a lot of credits for the recent growing popularity of tiny house movements but one of the most popular and practical ones was Surah Susanka who wrote the book *"The Not so Big House"* in 2007 and Henry David Thoreau who wrote the book "Walden"

After Hurricane Katrina did its devastating number and rendered many people homeless in 2005, a female architect known as Marianne Cusato from Kenai Alaska, then resident in Miami, Florida came up with the tiny house design by designing a number of cottages with an average size of 308 square feet. They were designed as alternatives to the Ferma trailers that were commonly in use at the time and were meant to provide a much more comfortable solution to a disaster ridden zone. These cottages were known as the Katrina Cottages and they received wide spread attention and accolades.

The Katrina Cottages

2

Tiny House

As the financial crisis of 2007 -2008 spread, the idea of downsizing to smaller homes became more popular. People thought tiny houses were much more available and since they were sometimes built with cheap and safe materials, they were thought to be ecologically friendly too.

As the trend continued to grow and become popular, safety issues became a source of concern. This led to the formation of the American Tiny House Association, an association which was formed to provide guidelines and checks for the construction of tiny homes so as to avoid dangers that may result from non-adherence to safe and quality procedures in construction of tiny houses.

It is important to note that the tiny house movement is not just limited to America alone. Many people from all over the world are increasingly buying into this trend. Japan, Tokyo, Spain, Britain, Manchester, Germany and Russia are just a few of the places where the tiny house movement has also begun to gain more momentum.

Chapter 2: Why Live in a Tiny House? The Pros and Cons

We spent the last chapter talking about how small houses came to be and I'm very sure that by now, you are already excited about the prospect of living in a tiny home. However, just before you start packing your things up and getting ready for the move, it is important for you to understand some of the benefits and of course, challenges that would come with joining the tiny homes movement.

Benefits of Living in Tiny Houses

1. **Very Cheap to Build:** Building a regular home is no mean feat. The cost of building a regular home can be as high as $256,000 to millions of dollars of which you would have to continue to spend more money to maintain the house but tiny homes are extremely cheap to build. Depending on how good you are with your hands, you can build it yourself or if you can't, you can hire tiny home designers who can help you design and build the house for cheap. What you mostly need to spend on are the materials and with an average of $19,000 - $50,000, you would have a very comfortable and functional home to call your own.

2. **You Can Be Debt Free:** The bulk of debts that most people owe during their lifetimes are in mortgages. Many people have found themselves neck deep in debt due to the quest to join the league of homeowners. However, people who have joined

4

the tiny house movement generally have less debt on their neck due to the absence of mortgage debts.

3. **Less Money is Spent on Decorating and Furnishing:** When you build/buy a large home, you're not going to leave it empty, are you? Of course, you would want to spend some money to make the whole place look good. This is yet another way that tiny homes would help to stretch your financial resources because you would only have to spend minimal money to pretty up the place and make it comfortable for yourself and your family. Even if you decide to redecorate your home in a few years, it's still going to be easier and cheaper for you to do so.

4. **More Energy Savings**: Energy savings is a hot topic amongst homeowners and there have been a lot of inventions and methods that are designed to help increase energy savings and reduce energy consumption but the best invention yet is a tiny home. When you move into a tiny home, your energy needs would become extremely small. For your heating and cooling, you would be able to make use of smaller appliances, which would consume less power. You could even make use of solar energy much more efficiently!

5. **Cheaper Cleaning Costs**: Of course, the larger your house, the more money you would have to offer your cleaner so if you downsize to a smaller

home, you would be able to spend less money both on cleaning service providers and cleaning materials. And if you do your house cleaning yourself, you would be able to save a lot of time and energy as smaller homes are easier to clean.

6. **You Can Travel With Your Home**: Imagine having a business meeting in the next city or a few cities away and you just get into your tiny home, which is actually built on a trailer and off you go; there's absolutely no need to pack stuffs or spend money on fancy hotels! Yeah, such is the fantastic lifestyle tiny home owners enjoy.

7. **Less Clutter**: Clutter is a serious problem for most people. The statistics for people, who live in untidy homes as a result of too much clutter, are really high. People are suffering from mental and emotional stress due to excessive clutter in their homes but this is something a tiny house owner would know nothing about because they tend to discipline themselves to live with less stuff knowing that they have minimal space to spare. Also, living in a tiny house would help you to live a tidy life much more easily.

8. **Moving is Easy**: People often hold back on purchasing new homes because of the amount of hard work, stress and financial investment that would have to go into moving into a new home. So they continue to cope with unfavorable living

conditions; annoying neighbors, loud neighborhood, a house that is too far from work-they continue to manage these conditions because moving to another house would take a lot. When you live in a tiny house however, moving is extremely easy; it's as easy as looking for land elsewhere and driving to another cool neighborhood if your home is built on a trailer.

9. **You Can be Pro-Environment**: Most of the materials used to build tiny homes are recycled or salvaged materials, which mean that you are able to contribute your own quota to ecological advancement by preventing new materials from being made and avoiding the use of hazardous and toxic materials.

10. **Helps Your Family to Bond Better**: Because of lesser rooms and spaces in tiny homes, social interaction is improved and family members are able to spend more time together and bond better.

11. **Helps to Curb Spending**: Yeah, it's still about the Benjamins... When you know that you have no space to store things, you would be less tempted to buy them and this is how you are able to save yourself some money, which would rather have been spent accumulating unnecessary stuff.

12. **Easier To Sell**: When you finally decide that it's time for you to sell off your home maybe to move to another tiny house, you would find a wider market

because for one, tiny houses are very affordable to a larger group of people and also because a lot of people are leaning towards tiny homes nowadays.

These are only some of the benefits you would derive when you move into a smaller home as its better experienced than described. However, I would be speaking with my tongue in my cheek if I tell you that living in tiny homes is a bed of roses without challenges. Of course, there are some challenges that come with making this bold move.

Challenges of Living in Tiny Homes

1. **The Move Is Tough:** The toughest challenge you're going to have is when you're moving to your new home for the first time. If you're going to be moving from a really big home, you would have to decide on what to do with all the stuff you have acquired over the years because obviously, they are not all going to fit into your new home. So if you've developed an emotional attachment to your stuff, you may have a very hard time letting go.

2. **You Might Develop OCD!:** Okay, that's me exaggerating but living in a tiny home means that you have to be clean and this means spending a lot of time cleaning because you literally have to clean after yourself. Because of the size of your home, it becomes impracticable to leave your cleaning for later except of course if you have no problem living in an unclean home.

3. **Tiny Homes are Best Suited to Smaller Families:** If you have a very large family, living in a tiny home might not be practical for you because there might not be enough space. Tiny homes are best for a family of not more than four people otherwise you might begin to feel choked up.

4. **Less Space for Entertainment**: If you are the type who really loves to host your friends, host parties and get-togethers in your home, you might have a hard time with this when you move to your new home, as there would be less space for you to host these parties due to the size of your new home.

5. **You May Find It Boring**: If you are the type of person who likes large spaces and find the ability to walk around your home and move from room to room entertaining, you may have a hard time adjusting to this new life of limited spaces. What's that word again? Yes, Claustrophobia!

6. **Too Many Critics**: The tiny house movement is relatively new and many people are yet to buy into the idea so you may have to deal with critics who would have negative things to say about your decision to downsize. The most challenging thing is that these people may be your close friends and family. And oh, let's not forget the stares from people who would think you've gone crazy for daring to do this.

7. **You Need a Lot of Time and Energy to Build**: Though they are tiny homes, the efforts and time that go into getting them together are not tiny. Most tiny homeowners build their homes themselves and this takes a lot of time and effort.

8. **Working From Home Might Be a Challenge**: There might be no space for a home office and this might be challenging for people who have to work from home.

9. **You're Going To Have a Small Kitchen**: I know that a lot of people, especially women, love large kitchens. It's even a thing of pride and something to show off in some societies but with your tiny home, you would have to kiss your dreams of a large kitchen goodbye because tiny homes come with tiny but functional kitchens.

10. **Less Space for Storage:** I don't know if this is actually a benefit or a downsize but the thing is, you may have to rent an extra storage space if you want to hold on to some of your stuffs from your former home because there is typically less space for storage when you live in a tiny home.

11. **Health Concerns**: There are also some health concerns that tiny homes can promote the quick spread of diseases and epidemics due to less breathing space available.

12. **Composting Toilets**: The toilet in your tiny home is going to be slightly different from what you are used to. You would have to make use of composting toilets, which might take some getting used to.

13. **Obtaining Loans is Challenging**: You know the thing with new innovations; people typically do not trust them in the beginning and this is what is happening with financial institutions; they do not believe that tiny houses have good resale value and would typically hold back on handing out a loan for building one. Therefore, if you are considering building a tiny home with credit facility from your financial institution, you may face a slight brick wall there. In fact, you just may have to pay with cash.

14. **Tiny Houses and the Law**: When it comes to zoning laws and building codes, the issue of tiny homes is still a grey area. Many a tiny homeowners find themselves being harassed and disturbed by law enforcement agents as a result of this. However, in this book, I have taken out time to explain, in details, the issue of zoning and how you can avoid run-ins with law enforcement agents.

15. **Land Acquisition**: You don't need a lot of land to build your time home on but you still need some space and this might cost you a lot if you live in the city centers or in expensive areas.

In spite of these challenges, you would agree with me that the advantages of living in tiny homes far outweigh the disadvantages and tiny house living is a win-win situation at the end of the day.

The next chapter describes in detail, what a tiny home is and what it is not.

Chapter 3: Living in a Tiny House- What it is and What it is Not

Before we move further, it is important for you to get a full picture of what a tiny house is as well as to discuss some of the misconceptions about tiny houses. At the end of this chapter, you would be able to get a deeper and clearer picture of what a tiny house should be and what it is not.

So what exactly is a Tiny House?

A tiny house is a house that is between 100 -400 square feet in size. This is at least 6 to 7 times smaller than the typical American home. However, some tiny homes can be as large as 1,000 square feet in size. Tiny homes could be built on wheels (on a trailer) or on land and they can come in different shapes, sizes and form.

A Tiny House on a Wheel

A Tiny House Built on Land

Tiny homes would usually contain sleeping areas, living area, bathrooms and of course, a kitchen and they are built to be self-contained, off-the-grid and able to generate their own water and electricity.

What does it really feel like to live in a Tiny House?

It is only normal that you would want to know what it really feels like to live in a tiny home before you make the leap. You've probably seen photos of tiny homes and you admired it very much but photos don't always tell the whole story; do they?

- **You Have to Be Ready to Work**: Tiny homes get cluttered real quick and for you to keep it clean and enjoyable, you have to be ready to work and you must be disciplined enough to be able to put everything in its place after every use. Messy places can cause discomfort and anxiety so if you do not want to deal with that, you must come up with a regular routine for picking after yourself and returning things back in their place. In short, there is really no room for laziness or dirtiness in a tiny home.

- **No Space for Many Guests**: If you are the type who loves to entertain many guests, you may have to adjust your socialization strategy because hosting many guests in your home would be practically impossible.

- **Less Stress and More Contentment**: As soon as you get used to picking after yourself and you have developed a schedule for keeping things clean, you will feel less stressed because you would be living a minimalist lifestyle where you would have to deal less stuff. Moreover, you will not feel the need to acquire excess stuff to validate yourself. You will have just the basics that you need and you would be content with what you have.

Common Misconceptions about Tiny Houses

- **People Who Live in Tiny Houses are Poor or Unemployed**

Don't be surprised when you tell people that you have a job and they find it very hard to believe you because the general belief is that people who live in tiny houses are either poor or unemployed. The truth is that people don't live in tiny homes because they are poor; in fact, most people who live in tiny houses are gainfully employed and not less privileged like a lot of people like to think.

- **It's Impossible to Build a Family in a Tiny House**

Another misconception is that you cannot have a relationship or raise a family in a tiny home but there are lots of examples of tiny house owners who live in it with their family and have solid relationships too. Although it is difficult or practically impossible to raise a very large family in a tiny home, you can still live in it if your family is relatively small.

- **Tiny Houses are Not Real Houses**

Another misconception is that a tiny house is just a camper and not a real house. Well, a tiny house is a real house and has all the facilities that a large house would have such as electricity, toilet, shower, kitchen, bathroom and every other facility. Tiny houses are also built the same way and built with the same materials as large houses so why would anyone say it's not a real house?

- **You Can't Privacy in a Tiny House**

It's possible to have privacy in your tiny house. First, you can use sliding doors or pocket doors to close off the spaces where you would need privacy. Moreover, if you respect one another's privacy, there shouldn't be any privacy issues.

- **You Must Be Handy/ DIY**

You don't have to be good with your hands or DIY anything; you can hire people to do all the work! There are tiny house owners who choose to handle everything themselves because they have the skills and there are also some tiny house owners who know nothing about home construction and instead hire other people to do it for them.

- **You Have to Give Up All Your Stuff**

The tiny house living is not about becoming a monk or a hobo; you don't have to give up all your stuff to join the movement. However, you do have to set some priorities. You have to decide on what is important and what is not and everything you acquire must have a use; it's goodbye to those days when you just acquire stuff because it is trending or because everyone else is doing so. You acquire things because you need them and you get rid of them as soon as you no longer have need for them.

Now that you have a clear picture of what the tiny life looks and feels like, it's time to start planning your own tiny house. The next chapter will reveal all the steps you need to take before you start building your tiny home.

Chapter 4: Factors to Consider Before Building a Tiny House

Moving to a tiny house is often paraded as something that is very easy to do and a kind of resort for when you have financial problems but it's not always as easy as it looks. There are many factors that have to be put into consideration. A few of them will be discussed below:

Personal Goals

First, you have to consider your goals for wanting to join the tiny house movement. The reasons why people choose to live in a tiny home differ and are not just financial. I have heard of some people who decided to join the tiny house movement in order to get healing from some type of diseases and there are also stories about people who decided to do it as a way to improve their relationships and bond better.

So first, you have to consider why you want to join the tiny house movement and find out if there are any better alternatives. For instance, if you want to cut back on your rent, you may not need to join the tiny house movement to do that. You could simply find out if there are any cheaper alternatives to explore.

This point is very important because you don't want to join the tiny house movement for the wrong reasons and end up frustrated with your choices at the end of the day.

Renting Before Buying

It helps to rent a tiny house and live in one for a short while before you go ahead to build or buy one. This would give you a feel of what it would be like to live in a tiny home and if you don't like it, you can simply axe the idea. It's smarter to go this route than buying or building only to discover that you don't really like living in your new home. So on your next holiday, consider renting a trailer to live in instead of staying in a hotel.

To Build or To Buy

Another important factor to consider is whether you would prefer to build your tiny house from the scratch or buy one that has already been built. This is a decision that you have to make whilst giving consideration to a number of factors as well as the pros and cons of each option.

Advantages of Building Your Tiny Home

- You would be able to save yourself some money- a couple of thousands of dollars, which would rather have been spent in labor costs could be saved when you build your tiny house yourself.

- You would be able to learn new skills and develop existing ones as you carry out the building project.

- You would have a deep sense of accomplishment and would feel proud of yourself for being able to build your own home.

- You don't have to worry about mortgages or any extra debt to own your house.

- You can put a personal touch to your home and make it into exactly what you want it to be. You would also be able to carry out repairs yourself, which makes the entire experience very cheap for you.

- You can control the costs of building your home and avoid any surprise or unplanned expenditure.

- You would also be able to have full control over the design of your home.

Disadvantages of Building Your Tiny House

- You need to invest a lot of time into building the house. You may be able to save a lot of money but you also have to sacrifice some of your favorite activities to be able to have enough time to complete construction of the house.

- You also need a lot of physical energy and stamina to be able to put things together.

- Building your tiny house yourself can also be emotionally exhausting and overwhelming. It could also put a strain on your relationships due to the time and energy investment that it would require.

- You can't compare the work of a professional to what you would do hence the quality of your home could end up lower than what a professional would do.

- A non-professional would only have a rough idea of cost so you might discover that you would have to deal with some surprise costs.

- Lastly, your design might be wacky and not as good as what a professional would come up with.

Advantages of Buying Your Tiny House

- You know upfront what your house would cost and there would be no surprises at all.

- You also have a clear knowledge of the specifications of the home and the facilities it would contain before you sign a contract.

- The house will definitely be built by a professional so your house would be built to professional standards.

- Buying a tiny house is also faster and when you buy, you would be able to move in to your new home faster.

- Many tiny house builders also offer warranties on their homes so this is something you can get to take advantage of when you choose to buy instead of to build a tiny house.

Disadvantages of Buying Your Tiny House

- You have to spend more money when you buy compared to when you build yourself.

- You might not get all the designs and specifications that you need.

Zoning and Building Codes

Every prospective tiny house owner needs to have an understanding of zoning and building codes with respect to tiny homes. This would help you avoid being on the erring side of the law and also avoid having your tiny home demolished after you must have spent a lot of time and energy to get it together.

First, what is zoning Law and Building Codes?

Different cities, counties and townships have their own unique zoning laws as well as building codes. However, zoning laws are quite different from building codes. Whilst zoning laws describe where your house can be located, building codes specify the minimum standards for the construction of your home. These laws are put in place for a number of reasons including health, safety and aesthetic reasons. In essence, zoning laws say this is where you can build your tiny home and this is where you can't and building codes state that your house must at least look like this or better. Get it now?

Requirements for zoning laws differ but could include a number of criteria such as:

- Emergency vehicle access for safety reasons

- Sewer connections for health reasons

- Rainwater runoff control for safety reasons

- Municipal or well water hookups for health reasons

- Minimum lot size

- Minimum square footage of houses

- Number of residences that can be located on a lot

These are just a few of the things that zoning laws cover. Basically, the law is meant to protect you as well as to protect the financial value of properties (land) in the area.

Therefore, you have to find out what zoning laws exist in the area where you want to locate your tiny home. Most zoning regulations recognize and make provisions for accessory dwelling units (ADU), tiny houses, secondary dwelling units and granny cottages. However, some of these regulations require that such homes be built on a foundation so if you have your tiny house constructed on a trailer, you may have to remove the wheels as soon as you park the trailer and then save the wheels for whenever you need to move in the future.

The most common challenge that tiny house owners who want to construct their homes on a foundation face is that some zoning laws specify a minimum lot size of 400ft – 1,500 square feet for residential homes. This essentially means that property owners have to apply for variances in order to situate a tiny house, which is usually smaller than the minimum specification. There is however no guarantee that your application would be successful with the zoning board.

With these challenges with zoning regulations, most tiny home owners settle for other options (which we will discuss below) but if you want to locate your tiny home in a residential area, the best thing you can do is to rent a house that already has a property on it and then construct your tiny home at the backyard as an accessory dwelling unit since this is totally recognized by the law. You could also look for someone who can maybe rent their backyard space to you for constructing your tiny house on or as an alternative, you can look for a township without zoning laws (some exist) and then construct your tiny home there.

Some people just ignore zoning laws and go ahead to build their tiny houses believing that if no one complains, everything would be cool but I wouldn't recommend that because you could be forced to move or fined at any time. It's best to just avoid the drama, right?

Finding Land/ Parking Space

The next thing you want to put into consideration is the land or parking space where you would place your tiny house. As I mentioned above, there are a couple of options you can explore.

- **Personal Land**: You can choose to construct your tiny home on a personal lot but this is usually a

24

tough call due to zoning regulations but if there are no zoning laws in your area, this is the best option for you.

- **In Your Backyard**: Most zoning laws recognize accessory dwelling units (ADU'S) and camping homes as long as there is a primary property on it which meets the minimum size requirements so what you could do is find someone who can rent their backyard to you or buy a property, rent the main building out and use the back for your tiny home.

- **Recreational Vehicle Parks**: Recreational vehicle parks or RV parks as they are popularly called are places where people with recreational vehicles are allowed to park in allotted spaces or longer. RV parks are increasingly recognizing tiny homes and some of them now sell tiny lots to tiny house owners. You can find a list of tiny houses that accept tiny house owners here.

- **Tiny House Community**: Another option that you can explore is to find out if there is a tiny house community around you. Tiny house communities usually have a bulk of tiny house owners already living there and they are able to sell or rent out some space to you.

- **Buy an Existing Home**: Lastly, you could just look for a tiny home that has already been constructed, meets zoning and building codes and then buy it. This is a great option if you don't want to deal with the stress of finding a suitable place to locate your home.

Family Size and Lifestyle

It is also very important to consider your family size and lifestyle before you construct your home. Some questions to ask include:

- Do you have kids?

- Do they have friends over?

- Do you as a parent sometimes need privacy?

- Do you usually have family over?

- Does each of you have different lifestyles- like you love late night television shows but your spouse doesn't?

- Do you work from home and sometimes need privacy?

These are just some of the questions you need to ask yourself because the truth is that tiny homes are not for everyone and your lifestyle, your family's lifestyle as well as the size of your family has a huge role to play in determining whether a tiny home is for you or otherwise.

Dealing with Your Old Stuff

Moving to a tiny home requires that you downsize most of the time. This is especially true if you are moving from a bigger home to your new tiny house. So the big question here is how do you handle all these stuff you've acquired over the years especially since it's not going to fit into your new home?

There are a number of creative ways to handle that.

- **Declutter**: First, you definitely have to de-clutter. You have to get rid of the unnecessary stuff. Look around your home for things that you haven't used in a long time as well as all those things that won't fit in your tiny home and then set them aside. Now sort them into three categories; those you are going to keep, those you are going to sell or donate and then those that you are going to store.

  Then organize yard sales for those things you want to sell or you could sell on sites like Ebay and Craiglist where there is a ton of people who would be willing to buy those things from you.

  It would be a nice thing to have some of these things converted to cash so you can have a tiny home as well as some extra money in the bank- win-win!

- **Rent an Extra Storage Space**: After donating, trashing and selling all the extra stuff, the next thing to do is to rent an extra storage place where you could stash those things you don't want to get

27

rid of. Don't attempt storing all stuff in your tiny home; it's not going to work out well.

Budgeting

The next consideration is financial- you have to know how much it would cost you to build your tiny home, furnish it and make it comfortable.

The best thing to do is to create a budget before you embark on the project at all. Here is a sample budget that you can use; you could customize it to suit your personal needs or you could just fill in the gaps.

Category	Item	Comments	Cost ($)
Planning	Construction Books, Tiny House Books, Learning Materials and Resources	To help you learn more about how to construct a tiny house especially if you're going the D-I-Y route.	
Planning	Designs and Plans		
Trailer/Land	Trailer, Tires for trailer, trailer wiring,	You could buy a new trailer or a	

	hurricane straps	used one. You could also buy trailer kits and set it up yourself.	
Trailer/Land	Registration and Inspection fees		
Trailer/Land	Building Permits and other Legal fees	Find out all the fees you would be required to pay in your locality.	
Labor and Site Work	Land clearing, foundation, grading and filing.		
Labor and Site Work	Roofing, framing, drywall hanging, septic tank, driveway construction, electricity,	The building plan you choose would give you an idea of the items you need to	

	plumbing etc	include here.	
Roofing and Framing	Metal roofing or shingles, lumber, structured insulated panels, felt paper.	Find out what framing components you would need.	
Windows and Doors	Loft windows/sky lights, living room and kitchen windows, front exterior door, back exterior door, closet doors, bathroom and bedroom doors.	A fire escape window is also a good idea.	
Insulation	Insulation foam and boards.		
Tools and Hardware	Nails, gloves, screws, safety glasses, saws,	This is especially important if	

	hammer, bolts, nuts, washers, joist hangers, etc.	you're going the DIY route.	
Electricity	Circuit breaker box, gang box breakers, wire, switches, wall plates, outlets and bathroom fan.		
Plumbing	Water heater, kitchen and bathroom sink, kitchen and bathroom faucet, toilets, pipes and caulk.		
Gutter and Siding	Downspout, gutter, siding.		
Flooring	Carpet, tiles or wood.	It's up to you to decide which type of flooring is most	

		suitable for you.	
Lighting	Living room and bedroom overhead lights, porch lights, kitchen and bathroom lights.		
Interior Walls and Finishing	Paneling or drywall, stairs or loft ladder, primer, paint, paint brushes, stirrers, pail, roller, door and window trims and baseboard trim.		
Cabinetry	Kitchen cabinets, bathroom cabinets, bathroom medicine cabinet, kitchen		

	countertop & backsplash, cabinet doors, knobs and hinges.		
Appliances	Air conditioning, refrigerator, heater, kitchen burners/stove.		

You could also consider hiring a professional tiny house builder/designer to help you design and come up with a budget.

Loans and Financing

For most people, the whole essence of living in a tiny home is because they can gain a lot financially. However, tiny houses don't come cheap. They are much cheaper than regular homes but they still require some sizable financial investments. This makes it impossible for some people to be able to finance their small homes out of their pocket. If you fall into this category, you may need to seek alternative methods for financing your tiny home. Here are a few options that you could explore:

- **Manufacturer Financing**: Some tiny house manufacturers offer credit facilities to buyers. Find out if there is one close to you that can allow you to spread the payments for your home over a few years.

- **Bank Loans**: Bank loans for tiny homes are very tricky. You may or may not be able to obtain a loan from the bank for your tiny house but if you adhere to zoning and building codes and meet up with the sizing requirements, you may be able to increase your chances of obtaining a bank loan/mortgage. However, most banks would not finance a tiny home built on a trailer; they would prefer to finance one that is built on a foundation.

- **RV Loans**: Some tiny homes manufacturers classify themselves as RV manufacturers so that buyers are able to obtain RV loans for purchase of their tiny home. However, you may need a very good credit and a steady stream of income to be able to apply for, and obtain such loans. You may also need to pay a higher interest rate of between 4 and 7% with a 20% down payment.

If your credit situation is already unfavorable, I would recommend that you avoid further credit and instead, save up for your tiny home.

Insurance

Before, it was impossible to insure your tiny home because the subject of insurance with respect to tiny homes was still a relatively new topic. Fortunately, new developments have made it possible for tiny home owners to protect their little havens against uncertainties.

A number of insurance companies now offer insurance for tiny houses as part of the regular home owner's policy. This insurance covers:

✓ Main tiny home dwelling

✓ Separate structures

✓ Personal property

✓ Loss of use

✓ Personal liability

✓ Medical payments to others

This insurance however doesn't cover for theft of the dwelling or earth movements even though they cover for theft of personal property.

If you decide to move the home to another location, the insurance company will have to re-rate the policy based on the current protection class hence this policy is best suited to people who have their tiny homes built on a foundation or a permanent space and not in temporary places like RV parks. Such insurance policies are now available in States like Nevada, Oregon, Colorado, Washington DC, Montana, California, Idaho, Utah and Arizona in the United States. Also, the average premiums are put at about $495.

Outdoor Spaces and Hosting Parties in Your Tiny Home

There are a few parts of your regular life that you don't necessarily have to miss out on when you choose to live in a tiny home. Parties and social gatherings are one of those things. You don't have to become a recluse when you start living in a tiny house as you can still have fun like you used to do in your old traditional home; you just need more creative ways to do so:

Here are some tips you can use when you need to host parties or social gatherings in your tiny home.

- ✓ **Movie Nights**: Get a projector screen, arrange some chairs outside or on the porch if you have one, hand out some pop corns and enjoy a movie with your guests.

- ✓ **Take Your Tiny House to The Beach/Park**: If your house is on a trailer, you could simply drive it to the beach, park or anywhere else where you can get some outdoor space, and then throw a barbecue party or something.

The key to hosting parties in your small home is to make use of your outdoor spaces judiciously. Obviously, your house would be too small to host a large number of people at a time but you would have a lot of space outdoors (hopefully), which you can always find creative ways to make use of.

36

You see that tiny house owners can have it all, right?

The next chapter is where you would learn all the nitty-gritty of putting your tiny house together and making it livable.

Chapter 5: Building Your Tiny House- The Ultimate Guide

I already mentioned that there are two ways to approach the issue of buying a tiny home. You could either choose to build one or decide to purchase an already built one. I'm going to discuss both options here and give you as much information as I can to ensure that you end up with a satisfactory and fulfilling tiny home at the end of the day.

Buying A Tiny Home

Buying a New Tiny House- How and Where, Factors to consider

If you're not on a budget or have any financial constraints, you can opt for buying a new tiny house because it helps you avoid the stress of trying to wrap your head around a lot of things; you just basically buy your house and move in. In fact, this is the best bet if you're new to the concept of tiny homes. If you're buying a new tiny home, there are some things that you have to put into consideration; where to get good tiny homes for sale and the important factors to consider before choosing the most suitable tiny home.

Factors to Consider

- Do you plan to travel with your trailer or move to another location in future? If your answer to this is yes, then you would need a tiny house on a trailer. This type of tiny house makes you highly mobile and able to just up and move whenever you like.

- Where Will You Put It? You have to have a land or parking space ready for your trailer.

- Size? How large is your family and what family size is the house designed to handle?

- Design? Do you have any special designs in mind? Would you prefer a custom design?

- Utilities? Which utilities are in place Electricity? Security? Water? Energy?

- Cost? A new tiny home built to standard would typically cost between $30,000- $80,000. But the prices would of course depend on the size of the home. The larger, the more expensive.

Where to Find New Tiny Homes for Sale

You also need an idea of where you can find new tiny homes to buy. You can find them in these places:

- www.tinyhouselistings.com: You can narrow your search down to the specific area or locality you want.

- www.tinyhousefor.us

- Tumbleweed Houses: This is a USA-based company that specializes in constructing tiny houses for sale. You can have them custom-make one for you.

- Tiny House Communities- http://tinytexashouses.com/,

http://www.uppervalleytinyhomes.com/Tiny-Homes-for-Sale.html

- Eco-Villages- http://www.dancingrabbit.org/visit-dancing-rabbit-ecovillage/

- Social media

Buying a Used Tiny House

Building your own tiny house from the scratch is a very good idea and an exciting experience but for some who cannot afford the finances or time input required to build a tiny house, buying a used one might be the best bet. However, there are some essential factors that you need to put into consideration so that you don't end up buying a tiny home that you would regret.

- **Reason for the Sale**: First, you must find out why this person is selling their home. You must ensure that the person is not trying to sell the house because of some legal or structural issues and that they are only selling because of cogent reasons like maybe their family has grown larger, tiny house living is no longer right for them or several other significant reasons.

- **Where to Find Tiny Houses for Sale:** It is also very helpful to know where you can find tiny houses for sale. A good place to start is www.tinyhouselistings.com, www.tinyhousefor.us or other tiny house online communities. You would be able to connect with several people who are willing to sell their tiny homes. You could also try social media, craigslist, Ebay, Facebook groups, attend tiny house events or subscribe to newsletters from tiny house bloggers. These are some of the places where you can easily find genuine people willing to sell their tiny homes.

- **Questions to Ask**: When you've found a prospective seller, you should be armed with a few questions that you are going to ask the seller, which will give you an idea as to whether you are making a sensible purchase or otherwise. You should ask questions like:

  o **Who built the house?** So that you can know whether it was built by a professional or an amateur builder. This would give you an idea of the quality of the house.

  o **What is wrong with the House?** You want to know why the person is leaving and why they have made a decision to sell the house. If there are any major issues with the house, this would give you a clearer picture of what is at stake.

  o **What is the Weight of the House?** If the house was built on a trailer, it is important that the house does not weigh more than what the trailer was designed to handle otherwise if you want to travel with the trailer or move from one location to another, you might face many legal challenges.

  o **Was it Built on a New or Used Trailer?** Some builders make use of used trailers when constructing their tiny house on wheels as a way to save money. However, it is important to ensure that the necessary steps were taken to fix the old trailer and restore it back to perfect conditions before building on it because if it wasn't properly restored, the house may not last very long.

o **Which Utilities are Available and how do they work?** First, you have to understand which utilities are available in the house and how they are set up. Is there a water tank; is there a way to hook up to the mains? Is there heating and electricity? What about hot water, toilet and ventilation?

o **Is the insulation good enough?** If you stay in an area with very cold climate, you have to be sure that the house is properly insulated and the right materials were used.

o **What Type of Electricity Does the House Have?** In America, most traditional homes are wired to use AC. This means that most appliances that are sold in the American market are also designed to be compatible with AC. However, some tiny homes are built to use DC and if this is the case, it means you have to purchase special electrical appliances that are compatible with DC.

o **What Items are Included?** You want to know what you're paying for. You want to be sure that the owner is not going to remove any appliances or installations from the house after sale.

- ○ **Location of the House:** Lastly, you want where exactly the house is located and how much it would cost you to get the house down to your own location.

Buying a used tiny home instead of a new one or building one can save you a lot of time and energy as you would be able to save yourself the stress of learning how to build one yourself.

Towing Your Tiny House Safely/Travelling With Your Tiny House

If you're buying rather than building, you would probably need to transport the house from the point of purchase to where you have chosen to situate it. Whenever you want to move or if you plan to be travelling with your house, you also need to know how to move it. This process is called towing and you have to know how to do it safely and legally.

- ○ **Tow Truck**: First, you need a proper tow truck to be able to tow your tiny home as it is impossible to do so with a small car. If you would be moving constantly, you could consider buying one but if it's just a once-in-a while thing, you could simply rent a tow truck for temporary use.

- ○ **Truck Towing Capacity:** Another thing you need to consider is the weight that the towing truck is able to handle. To be on the safe side, you should go for a truck that can handle at least 15,000 pounds weight. You should also go for large engine trucks with V8 or V10 engines.

o **Truck's Condition:** It is also important to ensure that your truck is in a very good condition in order to avoid break-downs along the way. Make sure you check the brakes, cooling system and very importantly, the truck's mileage.

o **Fuel**: Some trucks make use of diesel while some make use of gas. However, trucks that make use of diesel have been found to have more pulling power at lower speeds so you might want to consider getting a truck that uses diesel instead.

o **Legal Issues:** Make sure that the truck that you have chosen to use is properly insured, titled and has all the necessary licenses.

o **Towing Accessories:** There are a few things that you would need to be able to tow your house with a truck. You would need trailer brake controllers so that the driver can have more control over the vehicle. Another thing you would need is a trailer hitch to ensure that the truck can bear the weight of the house.

o **Weight & Load:** You must ensure that your truck is able to bear the weight of your tiny house. There are three major measurements you need to pay attention to:

- **Gross Vehicle Weight**: The gross vehicle weight is the total weight of your house plus the weight of all the belongings and passengers. It would also include the weight of the fuel in the truck. All of these would be added together to know the gross vehicle weight.

- **Belongings Weight:** This is the weight of everything in the house.

- **Dry Weight:** This refers to the weight of the house itself and the trailer that it is constructed on.

It is important to ensure that the weight of the load that the truck would be carrying is evenly distributed. It is often recommended that 60% of the total load is positioned ahead of the axle while 40% is behind it. Also, you should avoid exceeding the total allowed weight specified for the truck to avoid running into problems with law enforcement.

- **Condition of the House**: Another thing you would want to ensure is that the house is in a good and roadworthy condition. Burn off any propane, protect your windows from flying debris on the road and turn off your gas and basically, journey-proof your house before setting off.

- **Insurance**: Your truck definitely needs to have been insured but you may also need to insure your tiny house.

- **Routes and Parking Space:** Ensure that you already have a parking space in mind for the truck at your destination. If you're going to detach and attach your tiny home too, ensure that you already have a team arranged for that and also, you should ensure that you take the best routes where you would be able to avoid potholes, bridges, bends, traffic jam, phone lines, low-hanging branches or anything that may cause obstructions or pose dangers for you.

Building A Tiny Home

Choosing a Builder

Like I already mentioned earlier on, you could either choose to DIY, buy or have a professional build your tiny home for you. If you're going to have someone build for you, remember that this is not just some camping tent but an actual house where you would live in hence it is very important for you to ensure that you hire experienced professionals to help you build your home. Basically, what I am saying is that it is much more recommended for you to hire an experienced tiny house builder than hiring a random builder because the truth is that not everyone is experienced in the art of tiny house construction. A person who has worked in the construction industry for 30 years may not even know a thing about tiny homes construction!

Tiny House Plans and Building Guides

Just like when building a traditional home, you need a plan and design and sometimes, a building guide to build your tiny house.

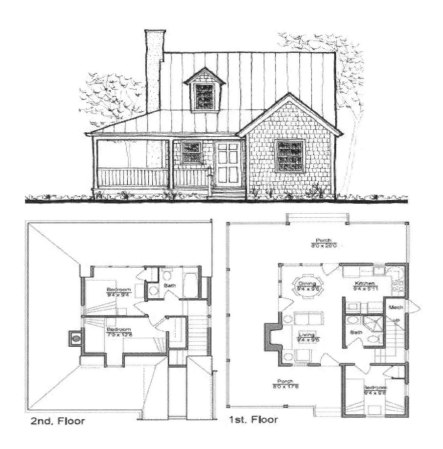

2nd. Floor   1st. Floor

What are Tiny House Plans?

Tiny house plans are architectural and structural designs of tiny homes that show how the house would look like after it is constructed as well as the designs, measurements and material specifications for the house.

This is a very important step in building your tiny home because it would decide how your home would turn out. This is especially important if you're going to be building the house yourself.

There are two ways to create tiny house plans; you can choose to create one yourself (if you have the skills) or hire a designer to do it for you. You could also buy ready-made plans online or get one for free.

What Should a Good Tiny House Plan Contain?

One of the most exciting parts of building your tiny home is choosing a suitable tiny house design. It is also a very serious decision because a wrong plan could lead to dangerous and costly mistakes.

Before choosing a plan, you should know what a good plan looks like. A good plan should meet the following criteria:

- **Be designed by an Experienced Professional:** Don't just buy your plan from a random place/person. Buy from an experienced professional

48

that you can trust and ensure that you do some investigation on the company/source before you make the purchase.

- **Features of the Home:** What features do you want your house to have? Does this plan make provisions for them? Don't just settle for a tiny house plan because it looks pretty in photos.

- **Framing Plans:** Some designers do not include framing plans because they believe that plans are typically handed over to professional designers who would be able to incorporate the right framing wherever needed but if you're going the D-I-Y route, it helps to go with a plan that includes a framing plan. This would help to ensure that your house is structurally sound.

- **Materials List:** It also helps if the plan comes with a list of materials needed. It helps you to get the right materials ready for the project and avoid unplanned expenses.

- **Cost and Time:** Again, choose a plan that includes the costs of materials and average total cost of completing the building project. This way, you would be able to choose a plan that fits your budget.

- **Exact Specifications and Diagrams:** Go for a plan that provides exact measurements, specifications and diagrams that would help to ensure that the house is properly built.

- **Used Plan:** Go for a plan that has already been used to complete a tiny house. Of course, the plan may look good on paper but how sure are you that it would be practical? It also helps to go with a plan that includes a photo of what the finished house would look like.

- **Includes a Systems Plan:** Ensure that the plan comes with a systems plan for electricity, plumbing, flooring, etc. This is also very important.

- **Sketchup Model:** The sketchup model allows you to make custom changes to the plan as you wish so if you're considering making changes to the plan, it helps to get one that comes with a sketchup model.

- **Instructions:** Lastly, ensure that the plan comes with instructions or a building guide that shows you a step by step procedure for constructing the house.

Where Can You Find Them?

There are a number of places where you can find plans for sale on the internet. I'll list a few reliable sources:

Paid Plans

- Tumbleweed

- Humble Homes

- Tiny House Build

- Minimotives

- [The Small House Catalogue](#)

- [The Tiny Project](#)

- [Tiny Tack House](#)

- [SolHaus](#)

Free Plans

- [Tiny House Design](#)

Tools You Need to Build a Tiny House

If you're going to handle the building of your tiny home yourself, there are a few tools that are necessary for you to have. Apart from your creativity and determination, the right tools are one of the essential must-haves for you as a tiny house D-I-Y builder. You could buy these tools or if you are on a budget, you could rent them from people who specialize in renting out construction tools to builders. You may or may not need all these tools but its best to have an idea of all the tools you may need and what they used for:

- **Air Compressor**: For air powered tools like paint sprayers and framing nailers.

- **Chalk Line**: Used to create straight lines so that roofing and paneling can stay in line.

- **Caulking Gun:** For applying adhesives.

- **Crowbar:** For pulling nails and amplifying elbow grease.

- **Chisel:** Used to finish cutting notches in wood.

- **Clamps:** For extra helping hands when you are building alone.

- **Circular Saw**: For cutting wood

- **Drill**: For making holes and driving screws

- **Dust Masks:** For protecting your nostrils and lungs while working.

- **Eye Protection Masks:** For protecting your eyes from dust, stones, flying objects and foreign bodies during construction.

- **Framing Nailer:** Makes driving nails easier.

- **Gloves:** For protecting the hands against abrasions.

- **Hacksaw:** For cutting pipes and nails.

- **Hammer:** Multipurpose

- **Impact Driver:** For tougher tasks that a drill may be unable to handle.

- **Level:** Used to ensure that everything is leveled and straight.

- **Miter Saw:** For chopping straight and angered cuts.

- **Pliers:** For pulling tough things off.

- **Reciprocating Saws:** For demolitions.

- **Rubber Mallet:** For softer persuasion.

- **Socket Wrench:** You would need this for bolting flooring nuts.

- **Screw Drivers:** For driving screws

- **Staple Gun:** For house wraps and roofing felt.

- **Table Saw:** For long, straight cuts.

- **Tape Measure**: For ensuring accurate measurements.

- **Tin Snips**: For cutting thin metal.

- **Utility Knife**: Another alternative tool for cutting thin metal.

- **Wire Cutter**: Useful when wiring the house.

- **Wrench**: For turning nuts on bolts.

- **Tool Box**: For keeping all your tools safe and organized.

Construction Guide

The steps involved in building a tiny house largely depends on a number of factors including the design, size, and location of the house you're building. However, this guide would give you an idea of the general steps you need take in order to build a tiny house.

1: Planning

- Decide on what type of tiny house you want to build- on wheels or on foundation.

- Buy a land or select a site for your home.

- Learn from other tiny house owners.

- Purchase/create a tiny house floor plan.

- Create a budget and purchase plan.

- Learn what the barriers may be and how to tackle them.

- Decide on the skills that are needed and try to learn some of the skills that you may not already have.

2: Buying and Sourcing

- Purchase a trailer.

- Decide on the type of windows you'll need and purchase them.

- Purchase the necessary tools and appliances.

- Purchase lumber.

- Decide on the professionals you'll need and how to get the best hands.

3: Trailer Preparation and Construction

- Prepare and level the site.

- Remove trailer decking.

- Remove any extras from the trailer

- Weld on the anchors.

4: Foundation

- Construct the foundation frames.

- Anchor the foundation to the trailer.

- Attach the metal flashing to the decking.

- Construct insulation for weather protection.

- Add vapor barrier to protect against water.

- Install sub flooring.

5: Framing of the Walls

- Build the wall framing according to the house plan.

- Ensure squareness.

- Test the windows.

- Make sure big things can fit through the windows in case they won't be able to fit through the door.

- Secure the framing to the trailer using anchors.

6: Sheathing

- Measure and plan the layout of the panel.

- Cut all the pieces appropriately.

- Ensure that allow for 8" expansion gap in between the plywood sheets.

- Test fit.

- Add glue to the wall studs.

- Use a few nails to tack in place.

- Screw every 3 inch on the edge of the panels.

- Screw every 3 inch on the edge of the panels.

- Screw every 6 inch into studs covered.

- Make sure the screws and nails you use are specifically designed to be used on treated wood.

- Raise the walls and anchor the plywood to the foundation.

7: Windows and Doors

- Determine window dimensions.

- Cut the window holes with a saw.

- Cut and apply house wrap.

- Test fit the windows.

- Install the windows.

- Tack in the screws.

- Test the window for functionality.

- Use the manufacturers' recommendation for securing the windows.

- Flash windows from the bottom to the top.

- Leave out the bottom edge for water drainage.

8: Roof Framing

- Install the loft collar ties and flooring.

- Construct the trusses as per the house plans.

- Make sure the height is less than 13 feet.

- Construct the headers so that it can be opened for skylight.

- Plan the layout and dimensions for the roof sheathing.

- Cut the boards and glue the truss edges.

- Use "H" clips in between the sheets.

- Use shank nails and screws to secure.

- Build frame for curb mounted skylights.

- Test fit and install skylight based on manufacturer's instructions.

9: Door Construction and Framing

- Construct door frame

- Construct or purchase doors

- Test fit

- Shim and secure.

- Install door hardware.

10: Siding

- Tape house

- Wrap seams

- Install furring strips

- Paint siding on both sides

- Hang

11: Outside Trimming Work

- Install the fascia boards

- Install drip edges

12: Roof Installations

- Install water/ice shield

- Install reflection barriers

- Install furring strips

- Install roof based on manufacturer's recommendations

13: Plumbing

- Draw out the plans for the drains, holes, inlets etc.

- Check under the trailer for cross beams.

- Plan for vents and 'p' traps.

- Plan for sloping so water can drain properly.

- Consider engaging the services of a professional plumber.

14: Electrical Work

- Draw plan for location of lights, sockets, outlets, fans, etc.

- Include plans for smoke and carbon monoxide alarms.

- Plan locations for HVAC and gas lines.

- Consider hiring a professional.

15: Insulation

- Install insulation and foam in edges.

- Install the vapor barrier.

16: Appliances

- Install water heater.

- Install shower and heater.

- Install Fridge.

17: Flooring

- Install flooring
- Cover with durable protection layer.

18: Walls

- Hang wall panels and trim around lights and edges.

19: Kitchen

- Plan out kitchen locations.
- Construct frame for countertops and cabinets
- Install countertops
- Connect stove
- Connect sink
- Install cabinet doors
- Construct shelving

20: Bathroom

- Plan bathroom location
- Install shower stall connections
- Finish bathroom walls and storage.
- Connect composting unit or toilet.
- Install vent.

21: Sleeping Loft

- Install additional storage

- Install lights and wiring

22: Main Room

- Install and finish HVAC.

- Install lights and outlets.

- Install any built-in units.

- Install storage.

23: Cleaning

- Clean the entire place, make it habitable and move in.

This just gives you a rough idea of how to build a tiny house. Next, we are going to discuss how to put several utilities that you would need for your tiny house in place starting with the toilets.

1: Toilets

When you finally move into your tiny house, you're going to need a effective and comfortable way to get rid of your 'wastes" especially if you're considering going off-grid. Unfortunately, this is one of the significant differences that tiny homes have from traditional homes- you may be unable to use a water closet system like you are used to except you have access to a sewage system hook-up.

However, there are a number of toilet solutions for tiny house owners.

- **RV Toilets**: If you've ever been in an RV, you would already have an idea of the type of toilets available in them. The vehicles usually come with a holding tank for toilet waste and allow for a minimum amount of water usage per flush. The tank would then need to be hooked up to a sewage system or emptied from time to time. Using RV toilets usually feels like conventional toilets that you are used to.

- **Homemade Composting Toilets:** Another option available to you is the homemade composting toilet. This option is quite cheap and convenient as it involves installing a large bucket with sawdust underneath a toilet seat. More sawdust is then added after each use then the waste is added to a compost pile after it goes through a natural breakdown process. You could also install a urine diverter in the toilet so that urine can be separated from solid wastes and odor can be eliminated. This method is easy and inexpensive, as it requires no sewage hookups or plumbing.

- **Active Composting Toilets:** These are quite expensive but very convenient as well as less stressful. If you choose to use active composting toilets, you should be ready to spend anywhere between $900 and $2,500 to install one. Active composting toilets are of two categories; the self-contained and the remote composting toilet.

- **Self-Contained Composting Toilets**: The self-contained composting toilets are quite large in size and are designed to compost the waste within the unit. They also come with air conditioning systems that help to reduce odor and ensure that the right temperature that would aid the composting process is maintained at all times.

- **Remote Composting Toilets**: The remote composting toilet feels like the conventional toilets in traditional homes. They are installed in the bathroom and come with a composting container that sits beneath the house or in another part of the house's exterior.

- **Incinerating Toilet**: Incinerating toilets are also great but quite expensive too. Incinerating toilets are designed to burn off wastes and then the ash can be dumped in the trash can. This type of toilet however requires a lot of energy to operate and can create a lot of odor.

- **Dry Toilet:** Dry toilet are also known as 'waterless toilets' and just as the name implies, they do not require the use of water or sewage hookups. A small bucket that contains an electric motor is placed under a toilet seat and each time the toilet is flushed, the motor turns the bucket and the waste is wrapped within the liner and a new liner opens up to form a toilet bowl while the old liner is held in a receptacle. As soon as the cartridge of liners are exhausted, you would have to replace it with a new cartridge. This type of toilet is quite comfortable and close to 'normal' but it is quite expensive.

You would have to decide on which of these toilets you can afford as well as suit your lifestyle and convenience.

2: Plumbing

Another major concern you would likely have about your tiny house is how to get water inside and how to drain out water from the house as this is one of the areas where tiny homes differ from traditional homes.

Just like with toilets, there are different options you can explore when it comes to getting water in and out of your tiny home.

3: Getting Water In

- **No Plumbing**: The first option is to have no plumbing system at all. Relax, this doesn't mean that you wouldn't have water in your tiny house; you would use water but there would be no automated source of water. You basically have to fetch water you need from an external source and store them in different parts of the house for use. This means that you would need buckets, bottles and other things that you would use to store water in the house. This method saves you a lot of money but involves a lot of stress as you would need a regular and steady source of water supply or you may even have to buy water regularly, which could be very stressful.

- **Tank and Pump**: Another option is the tank and pump method. This involves installing a tank somewhere in your home and then making use of a pump to circulate the water within the house. This method allows you to live off-grid but can also be quite inconvenient especially since you are going to need to be making trips to refill the tank and the pumps can be a bit noisy.

- **Hook Up**: This option is suitable for people who are not planning to live off-grid. You can simply install the types of plumbing that RVs use. This way, you can easily connect to a regular water supply or install plumbing so that your house can receive water through an RV hose.

- **Hybrid**: You can also consider using a hybrid system, which involves installing a plumbing system so that you can connect to a water supply and also install a tank and a pump so that you can always have access to water if you decide to travel with your house.

Again, you have to really consider your needs before choosing the most suitable system for you. Of course, if you're going to be travelling with your home regularly, the hybrid system would work best for you but if you have no plan to travel with your home in the future, the hook up system should work for you just fine.

4: Getting Water Out

Another important thing to consider is how to get waste water out of your tiny home because waste water has to properly disposed of for health and legal reasons.

- **The Grid**: The easiest solution is to connect your house to an existing water disposal system. This could either be a septic system or a public sewer system. You would have to install a drainage system similar to those available in stationary homes so that you can hook up to an external system. This would however work only when you are not planning to go off-grid.

- **Grey Water Catchment:** Another option you could consider is the grey water catchment system. First, you must understand that when it comes to drainage, there are different types of water. The first type of water is black water and this is used to refer to the type of waste from the toilet. Another one is the grey water which is water from your showers, washing machines, sinks etc. It's just basically any waste water that hasn't come in contact with feces. You would need a composting toilet for your black water but you can drain grey water into the ground beneath your home and redirect it where it can be used by plants and trees as fertilizer. However, this system is considered illegal in some areas.

- **Collect and Dump**: Lastly, you can collect all your waste water in a place so that you can dump it in a safe place when it fills up. For instance, you can install a bucket underneath your kitchen sink to collect grey water for eventual disposal. The only problem with this method is that you would have to deal with the extra weight and sometimes, the smell and all other discomfort that comes with storing waste water in your home.

Which Should You Use?

Again, you have to consider the prospects of moving around with your tiny house and opt for a system that works, is convenient and is not illegal.

5: Cooking in Your Tiny Home

If you are used to cooking in a traditional kitchen, you may have a few concerns about cooking in a tiny kitchen. The truth is that there isn't much difference between cooking in the kitchen of a tiny home and cooking in a traditional kitchen. However, there are a few considerations you have to make before building your home so that you can have a comfortable tiny kitchen.

Some questions you need to ask include:

- What would be your source of power- electricity, gas, coal or others?

- How much food would you need to store and how much space would you need for food storage?

- How much cupboard space would you require?

- Where would your source of ventilation be located?

- Which gadgets would you use and how much space do you need for them?

- What kind of storage system is needed for the kind of foods that you eat?

Another thing that would help is to talk to other tiny house owners and find out tips and tricks, which they use to make cooking in a tiny house much more convenient for them.

As for kitchen cabinets, there are many options that you can explore such as:

- **Built-in Shelves**: If you have a lot of space, you can install shelves in your kitchen. You can easily get cheap used shelves or build your own kitchen shelves from the scratch using wood planks or pallets. However, if you're going to be travelling with your tiny house, shelves might not really work for you.

- **Salvaged Cabinets**: Another cheap option is to buy salvaged cabinets or get them from the dump and then renovate them for use in your tiny home.

- **Crates and Boxes:** You could also use crates and boxes to store your belongings. You could fix them to some wood to create drawers or you could just stack them.

- **Dresser:** Another popular option is to make use of dressers and substitute them for kitchen cabinets. You could use salvaged dressers or purchase new ones depending on what your budget is.

- **Hoosier Cabinet:** Hoosier cabinets also work. Hoosier cabinets are like freestanding cupboards with cupboards, drawers and racks. They are like the perfect fit for yours tiny house kitchen as they have space for almost every kitchen item.

- **Bags:** Depending on how organized you are, you could sew some bags and hang them in your kitchen where you would use them store items. You could also include some pockets in the bags for storing smaller items like kitchen utensils and spices.

- **Kitchen Food Box Shelf:** These are very good for storing food items. They are custom made food boxes that you can hang in your kitchen and can be used to store all types of food items.

There are many kitchen storage solutions for tiny homes; you just have to be creative.

6: Hot Water

It is also important to know how to get hot water into your home especially during the cold/winter season. You would need hot showers during this time and if you have chosen to live off-grid, this can be quite tricky. Again, there are a number of alternatives available for heating water in your tiny house.

- **Boiling**: This is the cheapest and easiest way to get water in your house. All you need to do is to boil a little bit of hot water on your stove and then mix it with some cold water until you get a desired temperature after which you can pour it in a camping shower bag. If you don't mind the stress of having to boil water every time you need to take a shower, this is the most suitable option for you. You can easily get these shower bags on Amazon or other online stores.

- **Solar Hot Water:** If your house is going to be located in an area where there is a lot of sunlight, then solar hot water system is your best bet. You could easily talk to a professional about installing a solar hot water system in your tiny house, which you can use during summers as well as in winter.

- **Tankless Hot Water:** This method involves connecting your water supply to a device that heats the water on-demand.

- **Propane Heaters:** This is another heater option you can consider, as they do not run on electricity but on propane lines.

7: Security

If you have your tiny house on wheels, you can't completely rule out the chances of your tiny house being stolen. Tiny houses are quite an investment and they are becoming more popular these days hence the reason why there have been several cases of tiny house thefts. Apart from that, you also need to secure your belongings inside the house. It is therefore very important for you to secure and protect your tiny house on wheels from theft. Some of the security features that you can put in place include:

- **Hitch Locks**: Hitch locks are low tech devices that help to prevent your tiny house from being hitched to a vehicle and driven off. You can easily buy them online for less than a hundred dollars.

- **Wheel Locks:** This is another low tech device and it usually installed in the trailer's lug nuts and they cannot be removed except with a key.

- **GPS Tracker**: You could also install a GPS tracker in your home so that even if it is stolen, it can be easily tracked down and found.

- **Security Cameras:** This can be used to prevent intrusion and criminal activities in your house. With less than $100, you can get a security camera that delivers footage to your laptop or your phone for easy monitoring of your house.

- **Gate:** Another option is to install a gate around your home in order to restrict access. With this, you are able to limit chances of the house being stolen.

- **Alarm Systems:** Just like most conventional house owners do, you can install an alarm system in your tiny house to draw attention to intending thieves and burglars.

- **Mechanical Outlet Timer:** This system is usually used to confuse thieves and burglars. A timer is set to turn on the lights or make some mechanical noises so that it seems like you're home. Burglars are less likely to break into your home when they think you're home.

- **Dogs:** Lastly, you could get a pet dog that can help you scare away thieves when you are not home.

8: Heating, Ventilation and Air Conditioning (HVAC)

There are two common options tiny house owners settle for when it comes to heating and air conditioning.

- **Mini-Split Systems**: Mini-split systems require less energy and are easy to install. They are also ductless and they could also be zoned to cool or heat a specific part of your house. However, they can be a little costly as they could cost between $600 and $800. You would also need to hire a professional to do the installation for you.

- **Window Units:** Another option you can consider is to make use of window units, which are cheaper and easier to install. However, these are not energy efficient and they can be very loud thereby causing a lot of discomfort for users. If you are on a budget, this can be a very good option for you.

10: Furnishing Your Tiny Home

Because of the size of your home, there is a limit to the number and the size of furniture you can have but that's the whole point of living in a tiny house right, i.e. living a minimalist lifestyle?

But trust tiny houses connoisseurs to come up with something creative. Multipurpose furniture is the 'in thing' for tiny house owners. These set of furniture can be converted from a couch during the day to a double-decker bed at night and a wardrobe for keeping clothes. You can find such furniture at Ikea and other furniture outlets. They help you save a lot of space and money.

Mason Algarotti

Tiny House Furniture

Tiny House

Tiny House Furniture

Mason Algarotti

Tiny House Furniture

Chapter 6: Moving to Your Tiny Home

Challenges With living in a Tiny Home and How to Overcome Them

1: Organization and Clutter

Moving from a traditional home to a tiny house most likely means that you've gotten used to having a lot of space to yourself and sometimes, it gives you a little bit of room to keep clutter. But in a tiny home, you cannot afford to be untidy because or allow clutter because every little thing becomes pronounced due to the size of the home. However, the truth is that keeping your house tidy and clutter free at all times is tough. This is one of the challenges that tiny house owners have to face. But with the right tips, you can deal with clutter and keep your tiny house clean and organized at all times.

- **Create Designated Spaces for Items**: One of the most useful tips you can use to always keep your tiny house organized and clutter free is to create designated spaces for each item. This way, you would be able to see an item and say "This is not in its right space" and you'll be able to put it back where it needs to be. This even makes cleaning your home very easy.

- **Always Keep Things Away**: The first thing you have to do is to ensure that the places where you keep things are not too far from where it is used.

Your kitchen knife and chopping board for instance is used in the cooking area and mostly in the area where you prep your meals. Therefore, the right place for storing your knife and chopping board is in the cooking area, close to the place where you prep your dishes. This makes it very easy for you to find these items when you need to use them as well as return them to the right place after use. It is very important that you return everything to its proper space after use.

- **Digitize Your Books, CD's and DVD's**: It's 2016; do you really need to be piling cases of books and DVD'S? In a tiny house, you really don't have much space so you have to learn to make judicious use of what you do have. Instead of keeping hard covers of these items that would take a lot of your space, its best for you to have them converted to soft copies where you can store them electronically for future use.

2: The Cold Winters

Winter can be such a tough moment for tiny house owners especially those who live off-grid. However, you can avoid these difficulties by using the right tips to winter-proof your tiny home.

- **Insulation**: It is very important to have your walls, floors and roofs insulated with rigid foam against the cold winter days. First, you have to estimate your R-Value or have a professional do that for you then insulate your home accordingly. If you live in a very cold region, you could think of adding an extra layer of insulation.

- **Keep Your Vents Clear:** If you have vents that run through the floor such as water vents, it's important to protect them and keep them clear so that they can function properly. You could also purchase heated hoses and wrap them with heat tapes or insulation to prevent them from heating up.

- **Buy Dehumidifiers:** Another problem tiny house owner's face especially during winter is moisture. Moisture problems can lead to mold infestation and many other health challenges hence you have to pay serious attention to it. You can do so by purchasing and installing dehumidifiers in your home.

Lastly, you should buy double-pane windows for your house if you don't already have one and your heater is in good shape before the winter. Also, you should eat more of warm foods and drinks to keep your body warm all through the summer.

3: Privacy Issues

Another challenge that tiny house owners face is that of privacy. Some tiny house optimists are even concerned as to whether it's a wise decision to raise children in a tiny home due to privacy issues. The truth is that the level of privacy you would have living in a tiny home would be minimal compared to what you would have in a larger house.

First, you must realize that all tiny homes are not created equal; you can buy a tiny house plan for families and build accordingly if you plan on moving in with your family. Don't just buy a general tiny house plan as it may be designed for bachelors and single people and of course, you're not going to have much privacy living in them.

Another thing that works is to create sacred spaces especially if you have children. As a couple, you would need some couple-time to yourselves and you don't want the kids barging in on you whenever they want so it helps to create a space in the home where the kids recognize as 'mum and dad's' and they know that they are not allowed in whenever the parents are in there.

You also have to learn how to communicate with your kids a lot and let them understand why they can't do so many things like keep a lot of stuff or make a lot of noise like the other kids. When your kids understand the reasons for these things, they would be more obliged to cooperate with you and work along with you to make tiny house living work.

Conclusion

Living in a tiny house takes a lot of initial work and getting used to but at the end of the day, you get used to it and it becomes a thrilling experience that you want to share with others and talk about all the time. It always helps to join tiny house communities before you build or buy your tiny house so that you would be able to learn from other people's experiences. You would also find it very helpful to rent a tiny home and live in it for a while first before you make the big leap so that you can get a feel of what tiny living feels like (especially if you're planning to move in with your family) and decide if it's for you or not.

Thank you again for reading this book!

I hope this book was able to help you to know how to make the switch to a tiny home.

The next step is to implement what you have learnt.

Finally, if you enjoyed this book, would you be kind enough to leave a review for this book on Amazon?

Thank you again!

Made in the USA
Middletown, DE
08 August 2016